Super Hero Adam was in charge of naming all the animals. Unscramble these animal names.

SUPER HERO ADAM

OLNI   _____

ARZBE   _____

FEAFRGI   _____

AEVEBR   _____

EYKONM   _____

HAELW   _____

LEGAE   _____

BIATBR   _____

Read about Adam, the very first super hero, in Genesis 2

Color the picture of super heroes Caleb and Joshua. They trusted God to give the Israelites the Promised Land, even though giants lived there. They had a rock-solid faith in God. That's what made them super heroes.

SUPER HERO JOSHUA

Read their story in Numbers 13-14

SUPER HERO CALEB

God is faithful
to do what
He says.

1 Corinthians 1:9

SUPER HERO WHO SHARED

Which path must the boy follow to bring the 5 loaves and 2 fish to Jesus so that He can multiply them?

Read about this super hero in John 6:1-14

4

SUPER HERO JONAH

Jonah was very sorry for disobeying God. Asking God for forgiveness and then doing what pleases Him is the super hero thing to do.

Read his story in the book of Jonah

Connect the dots and help Samson to push down the pillars.

SUPER HERO SAMSON

Read about strong man Samson in Judges 13-16

Connect the object to the hero to whom it belongs.

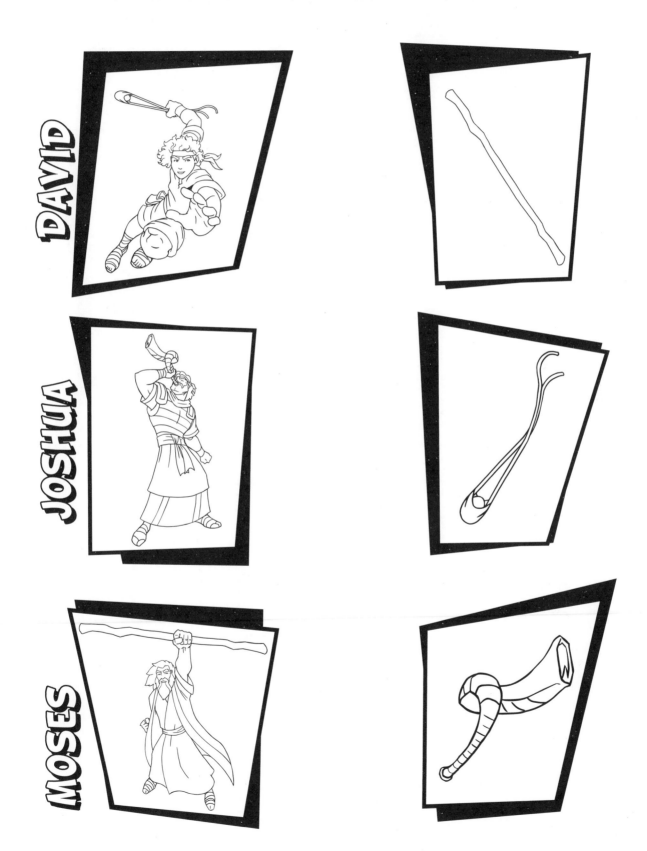

DAVID

JOSHUA

MOSES

Zacchaeus is taking Jesus to his house for lunch. Help him to make his way through the maze.

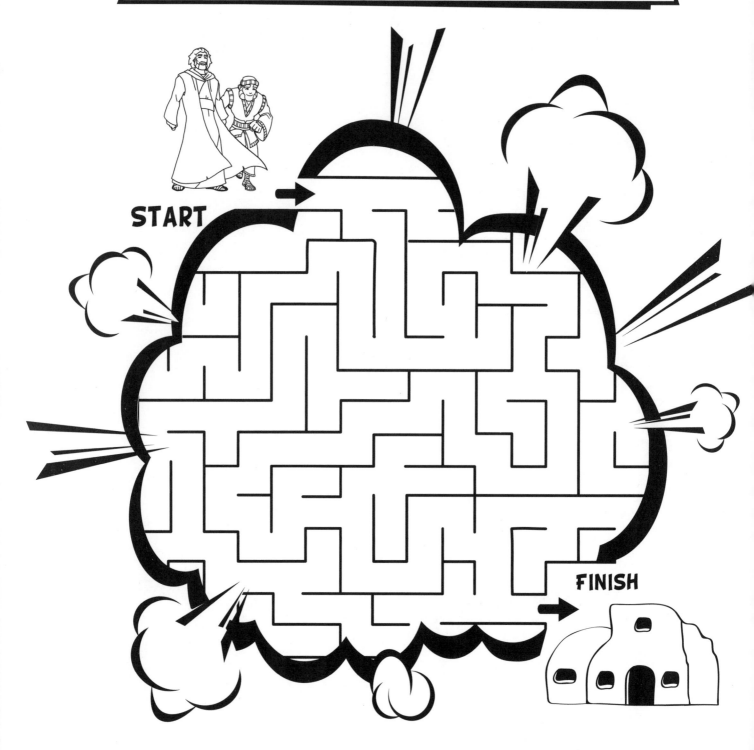

START

FINISH

Read about little Zacchaeus's big change of heart in Mark 2:1-12

SUPER HERO ELIJAH

Elijah obeyed and served God. He challenged the prophets of Baal to a contest and beat them!

Read about it in 1 Kings 18:19-40

Color in the colors of the rainbow

RED
ORANGE
YELLOW
GREEN
BLUE
INDIGO
VIOLET

God keeps His promises!

Noah was a brave, stormy sea adventurer. He went on a wild adventure with a boat full of animals! He trusted God to be with them.

Read about Noah's Ark in Genesis 6-8

10

Join the dots to see brave Daniel. Then color Daniel and the lions.

SUPER HERO DANIEL

Read all about Daniel and his adventure in the lions' den in Daniel 6

How many smaller words can you make from the word **SUPERHEROES?** Write the words in the shapes below.

SUPER HERO SAMUEL

Samuel was a super hero with super-duper hearing. He heard God calling him in the night and he listened to what God said. A super hero listens carefully and then acts.

Read about it in 1 Samuel 3

A	B	C	D	E	F	G	H	I	J	K	L	M	N	O	P	Q	R	S	T	U	V	W	X	Y	Z
1	2	3	4	5	6	7	8	9	10	11	12	13	14	15	16	17	18	19	20	21	22	23	24	25	26

8   15   14   15   18   25   15   21   18   16   1   18   5   14   20   19

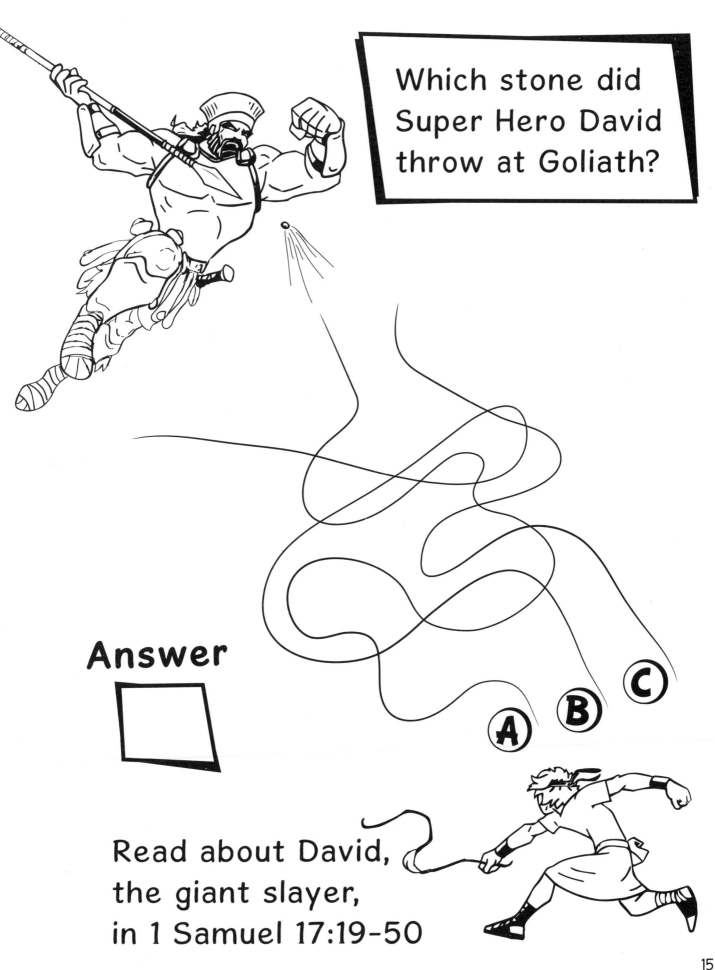

Which stone did Super Hero David throw at Goliath?

Answer

Read about David, the giant slayer, in 1 Samuel 17:19-50

Love
Peace
Patience
Kindness
Goodness
Faithfulness
Gentleness
Truthfulness
Hope
Holiness
Joy
Thankfulness
Forgiveness
Caring
Sharing

B	I	F	C	W	N	G	O	B	D	Y	L	S	L	V	E	S	S	K
H	O	P	N	L	E	Y	O	P	O	L	T	Z	H	P	P	C	L	I
O	L	K	O	O	T	V	X	O	S	S	E	P	V	L	E	I	P	N
L	O	V	B	V	F	W	I	L	D	L	H	M	G	O	H	A	V	D
I	L	M	Q	E	N	C	A	R	I	N	G	N	F	L	P	L	C	N
N	R	C	X	B	T	B	K	L	M	G	E	M	L	I	G	N	P	E
E	S	S	I	Y	J	P	D	F	H	R	E	S	S	H	Z	M	O	S
S	Y	F	A	I	T	H	F	U	L	N	E	S	S	B	V	D	C	S
S	T	E	C	U	H	O	B	W	O	R	Q	M	H	N	L	V	T	B
L	H	W	R	F	B	P	X	A	S	S	U	K	A	M	F	I	R	L
H	A	Q	L	L	O	E	G	O	O	B	N	L	R	D	Q	Z	U	P
F	N	E	B	Q	R	R	H	C	H	V	H	G	I	F	L	E	T	A
I	K	S	S	F	Y	M	G	E	N	T	L	E	N	E	S	S	H	T
I	F	U	J	R	Z	C	K	I	S	T	D	G	G	H	W	R	F	I
Z	U	L	W	P	B	A	J	O	V	Y	E	Y	F	K	L	O	U	E
Y	L	S	L	L	O	V	E	Y	B	E	S	S	K	T	N	E	L	N
E	N	D	Q	Z	O	K	P	L	O	V	N	L	U	F	K	G	N	C
U	E	W	O	L	J	S	S	G	H	K	P	E	R	X	Y	O	E	E
X	S	K	L	F	Y	O	N	T	J	O	H	A	S	H	G	O	S	Q
L	S	S	M	T	Q	L	Y	S	S	C	B	A	K	S	Z	C	S	T

Find the list of words in the crossword puzzle. These are the powers of a true super hero!

Solomon was a very wise man. Decipher his wise words by using the code below.

(ALL WISDOM COMES)

(FROM THE LORD)

Proverbs 2:6

A	B	C	D	E	F	G	H	I	J	K	L	M

N	O	P	Q	R	S	T	U	V	W	X	Y	Z

Read about super-wise Solomon in 1 Kings 3:16-28

17

Spot the 10 differences between the super heroes in the two pictures.

God asked Moses to lead the Israelites out of Egypt. He gave Moses the courage and power to do the job. When God gives you a job to do, He will give you the power to do it!

Complete the Scripture verse by matching the words with the symbols.

- 🛡 armor
- ☼ power
- ✸ strong
- ▯ strategies
- ✦ firm
- ◈ Lord

Be ✸ _____ in the

◈ _____ and in His

mighty ☼ _____

Put on all of God's

🛡 _____ so that

you will be able to

stand ✦ _____

against all

▯ _____ of the

devil. Ephesians 6:10-11

Unscramble the words to reveal the super heroes in the Old Testament.

ojshep   _____

smose   _____

mnasso   _____

didav   _____

monsolo _____

honaj   _____

Solomon   Samson   David   Joseph   Moses   Jonah

Unscramble the words to reveal the super heroes in the New Testament.

epert   _____

seujs   _____

luap   _____

ipilph   _____

uahcacezs   _____

onhj   _____

Paul

Philip

John
(the baptist)

Jesus

Zacchaeus

Peter

John the Baptist didn't want the limelight. He was out in the desert and told people that Jesus was coming. The greatest super heroes are the most humble.

Read more about John the Baptist in Matthew 3:1-12 and Luke 1:5-20

Copy each square individually to draw the whole picture.

Help the super hero friends bring their friend to Jesus by coloring in the alphabet path through the shapes.

L Z I E G L T P I
X Y O J P O N M A
W K S R Q A H L D
V U T B Y X J K C
G M W F G H I N F
X C D E T Z P E X
S B Y K
N A

Read about their super hero plan in Mark 2:1-12

When Peter focused on Jesus, he was able to supernaturally walk on water.

SUPER HERO PETER

Read about his amazing experience in Matthew 14:22-33

Color in the picture according to the numbers.

1 Green   2 Red   3 Yellow   4 Blue   5 Brown

SUPER HERO PAUL

When you believe the truth about Jesus, your life changes. Paul became a Christian and telling others about Jesus became the most important thing in his life.

Read about Paul's super-duper change of heart in Acts 9

Fill in the crossword to see the traits a super hero needs.

1. Endurance
2. Courage
3. Obedience
4. Faith
5. Caring
6. Power
7. Forgiveness
8. Strength

Philip was on a mission to spread the Good News about Jesus. He explained the Bible to people so they could know Jesus.

SUPER HERO PHILIP

Read about this man on a mission in Acts 8:26-40

Can you find the
path that adds
up to 5?

Answer sheet

PAGE 1

OLNI ——— LION
ARZBE ——— ZEBRA
FEAFRGI ——— GIRAFFE
AEVEBR ——— BEAVER
EYKONM ——— MONKEY
HAELW ——— WHALE
LEGAE ——— EAGLE
BIATBR ——— RABBIT

PAGE 4

Path =

PAGE 6

PAGE 7

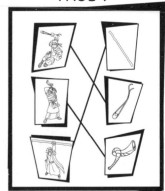

PAGE 8

PAGE 11

PAGE 12

PRESSURE ROPE HORSES PRESS RUSHES
SPHERES USER SPOUSE SHOES EUROPE

PAGE 14

HONOR YOUR PARENTS
8 15 14 15 18   25 15 21 18   16 1 18 5 14 20 19

PAGE 15

Stone =

PAGE 16

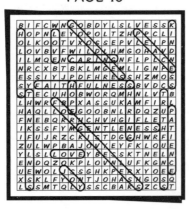

PAGE 17

ALL WISDOM COMES

FROM THE LORD

Proverbs 2:6

PAGE 18-19

PAGE 21

Be ✹ **strong** in the
⬦ **Lord** and in His
mighty ○ **power**
Put on all of God's
▨ **armor** so that
you will be able to
stand ✱ **firm**
against all
▥ **strategies** of the
devil. Ephesians 6:10-11

PAGE 22

ojshep ——— Joseph
smose ——— Moses
mnasso ——— Samson
didav ——— David
monsolo ——— Solomon
honaj ——— Jonah

PAGE 23

epert ——— Peter
seujs ——— Jesus
luap ——— Paul
ipilph ——— Philip
uahcacezs ——— Zacchaeus
onhj ——— John

PAGE 26

PAGE 29

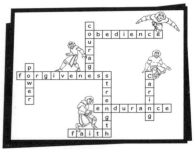

PAGE 31

1 + 1 + 1 + 1 + 1 = 5